UNBROKEN

FINDING STRENGTH THROUGH
LIFE'S STRUGGLE

DR. SANA ALI

NewDelhi • London

BLUEROSE PUBLISHERS
India | U.K.

Copyright © Dr. Sana Ali 2025

All rights reserved by author. No part of this publication may be reproduced, stored in a retrieval system or transmitted in any form or by any means, electronic, mechanical, photocopying, recording or otherwise, without the prior permission of the author. Although every precaution has been taken to verify the accuracy of the information contained herein, the publisher assumes no responsibility for any errors or omissions. No liability is assumed for damages that may result from the use of information contained within.

BlueRose Publishers takes no responsibility for any damages, losses, or liabilities that may arise from the use or misuse of the information, products, or services provided in this publication.

For permissions requests or inquiries regarding this publication, please contact:

BLUEROSE PUBLISHERS
www.BlueRoseONE.com
info@bluerosepublishers.com
+91 8882 898 898
+4407342408967

ISBN: 978-93-7018-125-0

Cover design: Yash Singhal
Typesetting: Namrata Saini

First Edition: May 2025

Introduction to the Author

Dr. Sana Ali is a highly accomplished medical professional with a Doctor of Medicine degree, a diploma in psychology, and certification in family medicine. Her broad expertise uniquely blends the realms of physical health and psychological well-being, allowing her to offer a holistic approach to life's challenges. In her thought-provoking book, Dr. Ali shares powerful insights from her own life experiences and professional journey. Her writing introduces a fresh and innovative way of thinking, encouraging readers to reflect on their own lives and avoid common mistakes that can hold them back. With a deep commitment to motivating others, Dr. Ali's work is designed to inspire positive change, offering practical wisdom to help people lead healthier, more fulfilling lives. Her distinctive perspective promises not only to enlighten but also to empower individuals to make better choices and embrace a brighter future.

Contents

1. Life 1
2. Communication 6
3. Love 9
4. Complication 13
5. Education & Complication 16
6. Anxiety 19
7. Change of Behaviour 21
8. Confusion 25
9. Toxicity 29
10. Relationship 33
11. Emotional drama 38
12. Mind or Heart 41
13. Finances 43
14. Marriage or show off time 46
15. Marriage Issues 48
16. Confidence 53
17. Happiness or just finding it? 55

18. Adjustment 59
19. Mental health 62
20. Identity crisis 66
21. Positivity 69
22. Meditation 72
23. Compatibility 76
24. Happily ever after with little issues 80

Acknowledgements 83

Life

Life or I say "what a life!" Everything looks good from the outside, but nobody knows the pain and loneliness from inside. So, now as we are talking about life let us say what life is- "A mystery"! Wait, you must be thinking that I am reading about mystery, but NO, no that's not life, for me at least.

Life cannot be summarised in one sentence and If I try harder, I can only say life is an experience, a passing moment. Every passing second is life, which never stops no matter how hard we try to spend each second, to make it fruitful. It just cannot wait, what we have planned, and that is called life.

By running after each moment to gain something, we destroy every joy, every peaceful second, every favourite music, which would otherwise provide us peace. The question is - are we born to run? Or are we born to live? And that is the part where it becomes painful, not for all but for most of us. Nowadays when people feel anger or pain, they just keep themselves busy to avoid the emotions.

Why? Don't you think, we all are becoming balloons that just need a little prick to burst. Why can't we just take a break, cry and feel those emotions, because they are our emotions and its a part of our life but NO, people do not want to face them. After bottling them too much they require a venting mechanism for stress such as therapy. Do you not think we are choosing the wrong way to deal with this issue?

A Lot of people think, *we have a job, we do not have time, we want to earn money*, but do they realise what this money is for? Let me tell few answers. Some say it is for comfort, some say it is for retirement, but do you even know how long you are going to live?

So, why planning this much and making it difficult just because you don't want to face issues. All you have are excuses. Money is for peace. Hence, work for money but do not give your peace for money. Take a break when needed.

Sometimes we think "IF I HAD DONE THIS, LIFE WOULD BE SOMETHING ELSE". Why wait for "IF I HAD DONE IT"? Just do whatever your heart says. Just say whatever you feel because by only sitting and thinking it is not going to happen anyway. What is this fear of failure? At least that failure is better than being stuck in the same place, at least with time you will learn to move on.

Now let us talk about if we fail- Yes, it is going to be hurtful, but that's only for a few days. One of the biggest advantages of failure is that we now know what we shouldn't be doing, if not what we must do. There is definitely some peace in knowing that every failure is only a step towards success, and that in itself would bring internal peace.

Failure also pushes away thoughts around ambiguity, which furthers the process towards internal peace.

But, will this failure lead to a perfect life? No, it is not going be perfect because nobody's life is perfect but, it will be peaceful and it will make us experience all sorts of things and we will eventually start to enjoy life with our daily schedule.

This internal peace is also something that ensure that we do not enable unnecessary emotions such as sadness and anger. Let's talk more about this in upcoming chapters of this book.

Life is very unbelievable, one moment we are little children, playing in parks and the next moment we are grown-ups, thinking about jobs and bills to pay. Life happens and we don't have much control over it. This lack of control could lead to stressful situations. And not everyone handles stress in the same manner.

A prime example is that of adolescent students. They tend to stress over trivial situations such as their love interest, at the very age of 13 or 14. It is quite normal for a grown-up, when they retrospect those decisions, years later but a teenager would not be in a position to realise that their response is triggered by their hormonal imbalance and that they are basing their decision on the footing of bodily changes.

Long back people were not so much vocal about it. But even nowadays, parents are not so much vocal about it with their child that hormonal changes happen. And you will start liking somebody but that is just a crush, you don't have to think about like marriage and serious stuff? And because of this lack, because of parents not talking about this topic, students come to a conclusion with their friends, that this is true love - Gen-Z love. Then when breakup happens, they think that love is not the right thing to do. And that we will focus on our career and this and that etcetera, but if parents have already told them about it, this could not have happened.

Parents needs to be vocal more about it. We will talk more about it in our next topic and in this book we will talk more about general topics which nobody is talking about. They all are talking from the surface, they are not talking from an inside point of view.

Communication

Communication is a wonderful key of expressing ourselves. But in today's world, communication has taken the meaning of being vocal about expressing thoughts and opinions. But, according to me, communication is a key which must be correctly practiced since the birth of an infant. It should be used by parents to build a very good rapport with their children and share everything and be accommodating of their children's problems, needs and wants. This would include communicating everything, share every joy and sorrow. This practice of continuous communication will enable children to be able to communicate well with others and in public as well.

But in 2023, communication within the family is very narrowed and considered to have its hierarchal space, in the sense that children are not encouraged to speak freely because they are not privy to conversation that happens between grown-ups. This type of behaviour can have its downsides. If parents or the family of a child do not give the child the space to communicate, then children will choose to get the same space and exposure from their friends or from other sources such as the internet and this could cause more harm than good.

The Internet space does not differentiate between children, teenagers or adults. It is a free-for-all space that allows everyone to put out their opinions freely without much regulation on what is being said. This in turn, might pose a problem when children have not been communicated to, about communication. If parents do not take the step to explain to children what and how to communicate and how to avoid certain type of conversations, the internet space will take advantage of their naivety, which would in turn lead them to develop issues such as anxiety.

The reason is that they are not vocal about their own trauma, about anything that makes' them feel bad, about any emotion, about any heartbreak, to the family because the family might have not given them the space to be expressive/communicative.

Communication is very important for compatibility because without communication, you can't develop any kind of compatibility. You can't understand the person. People say that after marriage you are going to understand the person, but what if you won't, then what?

This is also where communication becomes a crucial part to the extent where it can make or break one's relationship entirely. It is also important to note that it is possible that people may not be upfront initially in a marriage, but consistent communication definitely turn things around.

Love

WHAT IS LOVE?

Some have this, another has that definition About love.

What it is actually?

Let us talk about in simple language first. A special feeling of caring and being sensitive about that person thinking of that person to be part of your soul. In dramatic way, love happens between two souls, if we are to talk about romantic love.

So how do people move on easily from one to another?

It's just emotional dependency nowadays, to have someone in life to who they can share everything and travel and have fun. But is this love?

No. Love is a sudden feeling to see someone happy with you or without you, it doesn't matter. The person who is with you in your thoughts without being there the feeling of lights and positivity around someone is love. There is my favourite line by Ameer Khusrau- (credit- Ameer khusrau)

> *"Khusrau darya prem ka, ulti wa ki dhaar,*
> *Jo utra so doob gaya, jo dooba so paar."*

In English:-
"Khusrau, the river of love
Runs in strange directions.
One who jumps into it drowns,
And one who drowns, gets across."

It is so deep and so powerful. I can't imagine this kind of love or even put to words what intense love would feel like.

Love doesn't happen only by looks, it happens by nature; their nature captures your attention, making you want to be around more; that is one way of telling that you are falling in love. Your heart just tells you that its right. Love is like butterflies in stomach your whole life revolves around that person.

Love is a creator but it's a destroyer too. Some people get themselves destroyed in love and go into depression because they feel incomplete without that person. But they should understand, if that person leaves you that means there was never love from that person.

Take good memories in heart, smile, and move on.

You will have that satisfaction that at least you loved truly so don't destroy yourself. Live for people who love you like your parents, friends. Smile that at least you had that beautiful feeling. But I want to say this - in today's scenario people fall in love easily, but also detach easily; you can't expect them to last forever. One bad tome shows you there loves strength.

When they have no one, they will talk to you and when they have other girls they will treat you like a stranger. There's this man who has fooled till date 7-8 girls using the same lines. He is an educated engineer but most fraud person. You can't judge by sweet talks, they fool around. Using one favourite line I will explain love in my point of view-

"iss pyar me jo jal gya,
Samjho khuda use mil gya.
Tere ziker me mera zikr ho,
Fir hath se yeh dil gya"
(Credit: Qamar Nashad)

In English, we say:-

"the person who burns in love, they meet God. In communication, if talking about you is talking about me then my heart goes to you."

If you love somebody by not focusing on their physical appearance, but by the way the person is talking, that is called true love. Where there is no debate between mind and heart, the decision is purely by the heart. People get broken in many ways in love and we have many great stories about love it's just that if two people have such compatibility that they can build a beautiful love story then they should face the society and fight for their love. Love is a very precious thing. At this moment, only one percent love is present in the world.

When we meet somebody, our subconscious mind instantly knows if the person has a positive energy or not. When we get attracted towards somebody even then, our subconscious mind knows if it is going to convert into a very good relation or if it is just a infatuation.

Complication

Sometimes we make things complicated because we like to have a tough road, not the easy one. Decisions are what makes us better but I will say, some times it is good to go with how your heart feels instead of what your brain thinks.

We never want to hurt people we love, but sometimes we do because we try to avoid them to protect them from our situation and it makes things more complicated and its starts annoying us also instead of telling what we are doing we hide, to make it right, but it makes things worse.

Why cannot we take an easy step? Think from their perspective and do tell them. It will be lot easier and calmer. Yes, they can be hurt by knowing the situation but at least you will not have burden that you are avoiding and hiding and then it is up to them that they want to be with you in the worse or be outside for some time and give you chance to solve problem.

Human brain is always complicated because you cannot please everyone but we try and try until we hurt ourself very hard. First time it is going to be difficult and full of anxiety to tell the truth then the road is just smooth. Alone or together, you will walk out strongly, because courage is not outside, it was there always inside you.

Situations do not provide us solutions but there is always a loop hole in every situation. Universe has loop hole for all problems. Sometimes complications teach us a lot of things, because if it is easy, how are we going to try and learn about what to do in difficult times. Everything happens in life for a reason, we just must see it through a different perspective. No, it is not going to be easy but by doing this we can make things bearable.

Bearable won't be an appropriate word but I will say 'little less complicated' is a word. Stop pleasing everyone, stop doing what people want you to do, give yourself a break. Being busy is just pushing things deeper, it's not solving it's just avoiding yourself your emotions, your problems. It's not bad to sit alone take a break, feel yourself, face the issue and get out of it at least you can try speak out to yourself that what you feel and stop blaming yourself for problem, mistakes can be made by anyone, focus on the solution more than the issue and write down what you have learned from it.

Let me tell you what I have learned. I have learned to face it, write down my mistakes my problems and think about it from a logical point of view, instead of an emotional point of view, what I was doing till date because to solve it I have to understand myself first and forgive myself first. Then I can see clearly what to do next. I can't run away from destiny but I can make the path easy at least for myself. Our karma is in our hands, not our destiny. Destiny is always pre-decided. But by karma we can change a little bit. If you will look around there are always complications in everything - in job there are complications, in life there are complications, in education there are complications, you will find complications in everything; but you have to face it, you have to go through it and you have to deal with it.

The 3 main rules of dealing with any complication is:- look at it, think from a positive point of view and find a solution.

Every problem comes with a solution and every solution comes with an experience. To deal with the problem you will learn something with every phase of your life; someday you will learn patience, someday you will learn anger management, someday you will learn how to treat people, someday you will learn that somebody can hurt you so how to be not so much attached to people etc. Sometimes it is good to detach from unwanted people.

Education & Complication

L ong time back

In India, education plays a role equivalent to running in a race to get an award specially if you are in race of medical, engineering and MBA entrance exams. People are running because their parents want them to and they are running in this race since childhood without understanding whether it would even mean anything to them.

According to me, what you learn matters how much is doesn't matter. If someone like creativity, they should choose that field. Why do parents push them into something they don't feel passionate about, like coaching centres to clear a dozen of entrance exams.

They put their kids into coaching centres for competitive exams but don't ask the child what they want. Children study 18hrs a day to get a seat. If they don't get it, some of them are unable to bear the pressure and go into depression and commit suicide.

Suicide Rate is increasing in teenagers nowadays due to this educational pressure which coaching institutes also put.

According to me, follow a dream freely.

Do not think what people will say. Pursue your passions, you will be happy by this. Stand up to your expectations not others. Don't run, walk. Slowly. But learn accurately. Being like thus, you will always have two options - either I do this or that it makes our path easier.

Assist doctors or engineers to know whether you want to be like them or not. If actually yes. then do Smart Study, sleep well, meditate, don't take too much pressure, enjoy life also, because this age will never come back.

Now in 2025

Parents are saying whichever field you are interested in, take that. Don't take tension we have an alternate option, because now they are realising that its putting pressure on children and mental health matters.

That's why nowadays parents are not putting any kind of pressure on their children and when children think that they are going through a lot of pressure they talk it out to some kind of counsellor or some kind of psychiatrist to clear it up. See, counselling is a kind of thing in which by clearing up your mind and by telling you the solution things can be sorted by teaching you how to deal with it. It is best to see your counsellor, it is not a shameful thing nowadays to see a counsellor, every 7 out of 10 people are going to a counsellor.

Anxiety

People say it is a disease, but it is not. I will say it's a life style issue. And past trauma, sometimes childhood trauma. What has become a common sight is people self-diagnosing themselves with anxiety and running to the drugstore for medicines. That is not the correct solution. There are several other ways to resolve and maybe start from prevent anxiety and its symptoms.

For example, when you feel anxious, one thing you can do is start counting things or take deep breaths 3-4 times and exhale from mouth. Meditation of any kind daily is definitely recommended and most importantly, have hope that everything will be alright. The world is beautiful but you will find toxicity everywhere, you just have to develop coping mechanism apart from just being anxious.

The people who got anxious easily should not overthink things, divert their thoughts and meditate. It helps in self-understanding from inside so these thoughts won't trigger you. I saw one anxiety case, where the girl was always anxious due to toxic relationship so she broke up; that helped her permanently to cut off toxic bonds. These bonds can be friends, colleagues or relatives. Just distance yourself and believe you are enough for yourself. Just tell me what do we have - we don't have past, neither we control future, we can only control present, so live in the present any try to make it better so tomorrow you won't have to regret about the past. Do what you want to do, either saying 'love you' to crush or doing paragliding do it, you will understand the importance of being you, to make yourself happy. Happiness is always around you, you just have to open the eyes.

Do you know, anxiety medicines are so costly and so addictive and if someone tries to just leave it and not take any kind of anxiety medicines anymore, there are withdrawal symptoms, so if once you go through the anxiety journey of medicine, then you have to leave it one step at a time and it is going to be very difficult for you.

So, I will suggest that if you are suffering from anxiety, go to the psychologist. You don't have to depend on medicine, instead depend on therapy. If therapy is not working for you, you can take medicines but, don't depend on medicines because you have to learn the coping skills. You don't have to depend on yourself to medicines only. When you have the coping skills to deal with any kind of anxiety then you don't need medicine for it you will deal with it.

Change of Behaviour

After anxiety, change of behaviour happens. Nobody understands that what you're going through from inside, everybody wants to see you happy from outside.

There is a lot of change of your behaviour, you start being happy alone, you start being living alone, start being little stressed and little opinionated about everything, because you have gone through that low phase of your life that nobody understands.

Only you know how it feels, how panicky it feels to be anxious about anything, how much overthinking happens when you are anxious, only you know how much you have cried, a lot, how many sleepless nights have gone by and how many times you have felt suffocated that you have to go to the balcony to take fresh air.

When you are living with people, family, for instance, they want you to be like before but they don't understand that after what you have gone through you can't be like before, any they have to adjust accordingly because you are not psychotic you are just over emotional and you don't want anybody to instructed about what to do in life, and to do whatever in life because when you are alone and you are going through a tough face that face nobody has seen.

I know inside you are angry with everybody for giving you instructions on how to live a happy life and how to think positive but they don't know that any anxiety patient can't do it. it is a disorder and they are not doing it deliberately, it's just that it is happening to them.

They have already gone through a lot now and if you put any kind of pressure over them, then their anxiety might convert into anger, and if they get angry, you will be like – "why are people so angry nowadays? Children do not listen to their parents. They don't want to get into the phase where you see them anxious, because the person knows that the parents will be in stress.

With time, they will adjust according to you. They just need love and care and a little time to heal, a little time to leave them alone with themself to understand the situation, to adjust in the new change of place; inside they want to cry aloud but outside they can't do it because they can't show the world how empty they are from inside, they have to be confident and they have to show the world that they are confident about everything, they have to have a smile on their face every day but those anxieties are still inside them.

Do you know when an anxious person lays down on the bed they can't sleep and they feel more anxious laying down on the bed, that's why they are always walking around in the room. Nobody noticed this little change of behaviour in that person that even that person's legs are paining. they can't just lay down on the bed because sleep is not coming to them and they are feeling more anxious laying down on the bed they just want to open the window and have fresh air because they are feeling very anxious and therapy also takes at least 12 to 15 sessions to just make them feel little less anxious. And for the coping skills it takes at least 6 to 7 months of therapy and for that 6 to 7 months you have to try to be positive, try positive affirmations, try to meditate a little, try to do what you love sometimes.

There's the thought of paintings sometimes, there's the thought of just back to back and go on the solo trip but obviously your parents are not going to allow you to go on the solo trip if you are a girl. Three things parents need to understand – first, don't force; second, give them time to adjust in the house again; third, let them do whatever they want to do because they have gone through a lot.

Confusion

Confusion this word is more common than the word life because 90% of the time we all are confused either in a space of career or in a space of love or in general.

Let's talk about confusion about career, when we were in class 10th we got confused about whether we have to choose maths or bio or commerce. Most of the people who belong from a business background choose commerce because they have decided that they will sit on their business for the legacy, now for bio and maths, bio ones don't know how to do math, most of the people choose bio because they don't know anything about maths, and maths people know that they want to crack JEE to become the engineer they want to be to get the high paying job.

Rest engineers get in private colleges or the good ones who get good marks and get into NIT and get selected in good companies through campus selection and who get caught in the private colleges, they have to prepare their resumes and go to companies and do some work in less payment and then by lots of hard work, they get into good company. Now the time comes after two years of job when every engineer wants to switch their job so where to switch? Somewhere there is a 30% hike, somewhere there is a 50% hike. So much of confusion about money. Either way they will select the company which will provide them good money and less work. Now let's talk about doctors, I mean bio students; sorry to say this, but not every bio student becomes a doctor.

The good ones go to Kota and study hard and get selected in private or government colleges. Here, it doesn't matter if you are from a private college or from a government college, you should be MBBS or if not MBBS then BDS or BAMS.

Medical is a selfless job but those 5.5 years of college teach you everything from washing cloths of seniors to doing 18 hour shifts during internship in hospital. You become rough and tough and get so much patience that whatever happens you will stay calm. That makes a doctor very calm, soothing, very selfless.

After Medical College I bet nobody is ever going to get angry by a small issue because we have seen it all and we know how to react according to it, so when you have gone through a rough patch, you know eventually your mechanism and learn how to react without getting anxious, because medical is not a field of being anxious, it is a field where somebody else's life depends on you, so you can't be anxious about anything, you have to have presence of mind. Those seniors who give their clothes to you to wash it made you learn all the things help you learn all the things teach your patience.

And the ones who don't choose to be a doctor they choose to be either a pharmacist, or there are many fields in biotechnology, they choose to be over there and they are also working very well, they choose to be researchers.

So, every field plays a very important role in economy, every field depend on another field for something or the another.

You have to have patience and you have to have a positive attitude and slowly and steadily you will be able to get that success you need; with anger and anxiety nobody gets anything but with few deep breaths and calm mind you will be able to handle the situation and thus you will able to succeed in any phase of life.

In the first year of any kind of education, everybody goes through anxiety but they have to deal with it, Dealing is the main point. You have to be calm, you have to be composed, you have to understand that you have the potential to do it because you have chosen it and you have been doing hard work to be there, to be in that seat, so you will do it. Three main things you have to do in the first year of your college, first, whatever happens, whatever movement, anything happens, don't let that moment ruin your 24 hours; second, calm yourself before saying anything, think from future point of view; third, listen a lot, don't say anything until you have been asked because you will end up being in some kind of politics in the college, then you will be broken into two pieces, you will have to choose, so don't say anything in any topic until and unless it is important. I am not saying that don't take a stand; take a stand where you think it is necessary but don't take stand in everything sometimes being quite is wiser.

I believe you give them proof that you are right rather than saying that you are right.

Toxicity

What do you understand by the word toxicity? Let me explain in general, in our life everybody goes through the phase where they meet toxic people, now the question is how to deal with them. There is one problem in India that we have a habit of adjustment, and we think that by adjusting with these kinds of people these people will be changed but dear, let me give you an example- Lions' nature is carnivores you can't change it. That's how toxic people's nature are, you can't change it or if it will be getting changed either they want something from you or there is something good in it for them they are changing for their selfish reasons. Remember one line- when we are in dark, our shadow also leave us alone, so it is good to remember to never lose hope but sometimes we have to let go of these kinds of people who suck our positive energy and give all the negativity to us.

For example - In relationships also people are going through a lot. I have seen it - verbal abuse is there people are fighting but they don't want to separate just because the reason that one wants to adjust in every phase and other don't want to adjust in anything so why can't you see that there is no compatibility; it is just that you have imagined that I'm going to marry this person because I am in this long relationship with this person you are going to adapt everything even sacrificing your self-respect.

You don't understand that if you will get married to this person this person is never going to respect you because this person is not respecting you at all yourself. Respect yourself, your worth should be the priority, otherwise then you go through the depression phase where you try to kill yourself just because you think that you are not worth it. Sweetheart, you are worth it; it's just that this person is toxic, this person is negative, this person is narcissist and you are in the wrong relationship.

You have to move on and you have to leave this person before that person leaves you, you have to be strong for yourself for your future, you have to take a big step, take counselling, move ahead, be strong and put yourself first, don't sacrifice on anything because this is just a relationship even if you have been married to this person.

I would say the same that put yourself first. Adjustment is a good thing but adjust to a limit, don't adjust in each and everything otherwise people take you for granted.

I have seen it, some people are so successful, but they are running towards their partner and, they think that running towards their partner and adjusting in everything makes their relationship work, but for how long? One day, you will stop running.

What about that day when your partner will be gone? If there is true love, adjustment will come from both the sides, not from one side, respect will come from both the sides, not from one person. Liking and disliking will be taken care from both the people, you have to understand.

Be strong and take command of your life - you are worth it, you are beautiful, you are strong, and you know that. Whomsoever makes you feel bad or makes you feel that, you are not worth it that person is toxic; and you have to throw that person out of your life.

Be bold, be beautiful, be yourself, generosity and empathy is quite good but if it is harming us we should take a step back and we should protect us. Remember there's always somebody who can help you in any phase of your life and those people are your parents, they love you unconditionally and they accept you as you are. So never think about suicide, just think about better future either with somebody else or alone but without toxicity.

Relationship

The only ship that can sink anytime is called a relationship. Just a little humour. Nowadays situationships are more common than relationships. You ask somebody that what you guys are, they say that they are in a situationship means they are getting physical, they are into each other, but they don't want to commit to it; they want to see more options and they don't want to give their liberty.

What is a relationship or I would say what is a healthy relationship?

Think I know you don't have an answer or if you have an answer, you are not in a relationship.

Relationship is a combination in which there is love between to people to people share, a compatibility and a bond in which there is no space for arguments, big ones or any kind of, love it's just a beautiful thing. Don't you feel attached to that person so much, after relationship there comes in commitment in which people decide that they want to commit to marry each other. Most of the people who love each other a lot get married.

Now I will tell you what a healthy relationship is - healthy relationship is a relationship in which you respect each other's boundaries, respect each each other's workplace, respect each other space, and respect each other in general. You don't fight on small things you sort it out together; you have a sense of responsibility towards each other, you have loyalty towards each other, you are talking or you are not talking.

You know that, you have that person who is only yours. You know you both are committed towards each other. You both share a sense of compatibility, sense of liking, disliking and respect each other's valuable time.

You know what is important in a relationship? Attentiveness. If your partner is standing at one corner in the room and you are standing in other opposite corner at the room, your partner will be knowing that she has a habit of dropping her phone everywhere, she has a habit of putting her wallet anywhere, so he will be attentive that her phone is with her or not her wallet is with her or not. He is also enjoying the party but being attentive about his person he's in love with. Little habits matter.

Sometimes people understand each other without saying a word they are not like each other, but they respect each other's disliking also, liking also; and adjust accordingly, not only one person adjusts, both adjust. In the long run saying I love you doesn't matter, making people feel loved matters. Caring matters, understanding family values of each other matters. Now my friend if you have this then this is healthy relationship.

Sometimes people don't have a healthy relationship with themselves. We all should have a healthy relationship with ourselves first, people want to destroy themselves, putting themselves into a trauma knowingly; they know there is a hard road and they want to walk through it knowingly that it is going to be very painful for them. There is an easy way out, but they want to adjust, they want to go through it Thinking that they are doing good for their person.

That's why self-love is also important - first you should have a healthy relationship with yourself, first you have to respect yourself. Value yourself! This life is not going to come again, value each and every moment. If you will value yourself, nobody is going to destroy you.

That's why I say relationship is always not with people, relationship is first with our self, then with somebody else, that matters.

Five things you have to do on relationship with other :

1. Love unconditionally: There should not be any kind of condition in love, unconditional love with the purest form of love in which you don't want somebody to just be with you just love that person no matter what happened.
2. Pure devotion: There should be pure loyalty, pure devotion in love that makes your love more beautiful that makes your relationship more workable.
3. Being each other's best companion: Accept each other's flaws and accept everything. Love your person, fight with your person, enjoy with your person, laugh with your person.
4. Put your partner first: No matter how situation is no matter how bad the time is your partner should be your priority and that makes your relationship stronger.

5. Healthy detachment from unimportant: There are so many things that are unimportant in our life in which we are investing our time we should have a healthy detachment with them so that we can't invest our time in our relationship.

Emotional drama

We all have gone through this phase of life, where people are doing emotional drama over us. It can be for anything - in India 90% of work is done with emotional drama at families. It's a daily part of our life.

In work life this emotional drama is known as adjustment. They sayd you can't take leave because somebody else have taken leave and you have to adjust accordingly. We have two edges with each other now to maintain goodwill.

How much emotional drama is so much emotional drama nobody could have answered this before. I hope you're going to answer it one day. Scientists are also searching that how much of emotional drama is too much of emotional drama.

I know you guys must have been thinking that am I not emotional. I am also very emotional but I don't put my point of views or my preferences or my adjustments are whatever decision I have made I don't want anybody else to adjust accordingly and I don't want to say that please do it just because I will feel good about it.

I'm not going to say to my children that you have to do this for you to have to do that just because I have raised them. It is my responsibility to raise them not because I am going to have somebody who is going to just obey my decision.

My family has never been that emotional that they are going to say that you have to do it because we want you to do it they will always like whatever your heart says just do it and this is what my upbringing is all about whatever my heart says I do it I write it.

I want to give you an example one of my friend who was in a relationship for eight years. She was very happy in the relationship although there were ups and downs and fights in the relationship but she loved him a lot. She tried to tell this to the family and when she told the family, family started the emotional drama that your father is so ill and your mother is having this and that issue in health why? you want to get married to this person.

Though the boy is also a doctor, still he is not of the same caste, this is the issue, they don't want her to marry that person She fought for at least 7 to 8 months, she tried a lot, she cried a lot also. but nothing worked. Now her parents are searching for somebody who is of same caste but she can't love somebody after this long time, but she has to do it because of emotional drama.

Mind or Heart ♡

Mind and heart issue is from a long time ago - mind says from practical point of view and heart says from emotional point of view but our gut feeling says from neutral point of view and this is called our 6th sense also. If you feel from your gut that you are doing is right then you should do it you should not listen to mind or heart just observe the situation think from the practical point of view think from an emotional point of view and do whatever your gut is staying to do. Don't be afraid because if you will go wrong, you will learn something new and if you will go right, you will be happier.

Let me give you an example, one of my friends was in love with somebody from many years but could not decide that she wants to get married to that person. Just because of fight issues, she is unable to understand that what to do her mind is saying that these fights will continue, her heart is saying that after marriage everything will be sorted, so she doesn't want to decide anything about it. She is very confused.

I want to say if any of this kind of situation comes to you guys, you have to decide from neutral point of view. When you feel that my gut is saying this is right and I have to do this then you should do that because your gut feeling is never wrong; your feeling will say everything that will be right for you. Don't get involved in any kind of emotional drama. Just follow your gut feeling, you will be much happier.

This mind and heart race will go on your entire life. I just want to say that find your happiness - if you are happy in any kind of situation and you think that this situation is right then do it, don't get afraid that you are going to fall because if you are going to fall then also you will learn something new and if you won't, then you will learn that your gut was right.

Finances

Finances are a very important part of our life because nowadays people are very greedy; if they have ₹1,00,000 they want ₹2,00,000, if they have ₹2,00,000 they want more. There is always more and more and more; it is a never-ending process of having good finances; if somebody is super rich and you will ask them that if they are financially very stable, they say no, "we want this and we don't have that".

Tell me one thing – Does good finances give you satisfaction or happiness? I would say – no; it is much more happy to be with somebody whom you have understanding with or with whom you are comfortable with don't make yourself a robot to earn money.

Nowadays, students are also choosing the path where they get lots of money unless they should choose a path where they are more interested in. They think money can buy happiness but it doesn't if you don't have somebody to share your happiness with, money doesn't matter then.

I have seen it in NGOs that people with less finances are also happy because they have each other and people with good finances are sad because they are alone they have never tried to find somebody for themselves because they are were busy earning money. More and more money, more and more comfort is required nowadays according to them. According to me, if that money goes in the right direction and if you spend time with your family friends; do something new, give yourself also time, pamper yourself and give time to your loved ones, then that money is worth it. Help your family and friends then money will go in the direction that is good.

I am not saying that you should not be that kind of a person who are not earning a lot of money, I am saying that earn money have good finances but concentrate on your family and friends too because they are more important than money; concentrate on your hobbies too because that gives you the satisfaction, concentrate on self-pampering because that is also needed after so much of hard work.

Finances are an important part of life, but it's not the whole life. I have seen it, somebody with a very good finance and alone and just watching the TV late night; they don't have somebody to tell anything because they are always busy in making money.

They don't have friends because they have not contacted their friends from long periods of time, they are sad from inside, but they have lots of money in the bank. So don't be like that; earn money, huge money in a greater good, find yourself, balance with your money, be with your friends and family and be happy; happiness is more important than earning anything.

Enjoy your favourite sport, have a movie night, spend a beautiful dinner with your friends, these all things matter you can balance it out.

3 things you should do for healthy finances

1. Think from personal and professional both point of view. Evaluate the situation very nicely and then financially invest in anything.

2. Time management while you are doing financial gains - try to manage time for the family and friends.

3. Take out some time for your family and friends, enjoy, at least have four to five leaves a month.

Marriage or show off time

Marriages in India are very grand and it is visible in all cultures that exist across the country.

But in every wedding, you will see that there are 50 people you know and the rest 200 people you don't know 200. I'm telling you the minimum amount of people in an Indian wedding, they invite thousands of people to the wedding and bride and groom don't know any of them. Hardly they know the 20 of them but people want to show off - show off the best catering, show off the best clothes, show off the best things that they are going to give.

You won't believe that in Bihar, education of a man depends on the kind of woman he is going to get; that means if he is an engineer, then Rs. 20,00,000 of dowry is going to be given to him; if he is a doctor, then 50,00,000 of minimum dowry is going to be given to him.

Though dowry has been officially abolished in India, it is still a persistent practice.

So why do we spend so much money on weddings?

It is just a waste of money. I frankly don't understand why do we have to show off to these people who are from the society that people are getting married? There should be 50 known people in the marriage who you know, who you can greet and meet, who you have wonderful memories with, who are happy for your wedding and who know you both best. You should invite those people only so that there won't be any kind of drama, the more the people are invited, more the drama that can be created. You can't make everybody happy.

And then, the comparison begins that somebody else's wedding was grander and that this marriage is not that fancy.

Wedding as a ceremony is very beautiful. It should be done but at a small scale, in my opinion. The bride and groom should invite only people they know or only family members they are comfortable with. All the ceremonies and rituals should be performed in a very beautiful way, with less people so that less money will be put into the wedding, so that money may be used in other ways.

Outside India, weddings are very small with only 30 people involved, that too very close ones, and they have a very beautiful ceremony. So, to avoid any kind of judgement or any kind of wastage of money, we should also conduct wedding ceremonies at a small scale and stop the dowry system.

Marriage Issues

Do you know? 5 out of 10 marriages in India are in Japade Nowadays, just because they don't have compatibility or they have married each other in a rush.

They don't understand each other, their liking-disliking doesn't match at all. They lost their individuality after marriage because they have not discussed what they want and what they don't want after marriage, beforehand. Oops! Sorry I forget to tell you that in India we have two types of marriage - one is arranged marriage, the other is love marriage, but there is no guarantee or warranty that any of these will work out.

In arrange marriages, parents are more involved; nowadays, bride and groom also talk a lot in arranged marriage but that is very less, so they don't get to understand each other and they get married. After marriage, they understand that there is no compatibility in their marriage, so they decide to take divorce but when they talk in the house about divorce, people are like divorce is a very big taboo: "Nobody in our house in seven generations ever got divorced". So what? If nobody has had the guts to do it, do we also have to be in the same toxicity?

In love marriages, people know each other at a very deep level so they know each other's nature and everything, till after marriage there are lots of responsibilities and lots of things that we are going to discuss further. Due to these things, their marriages break and now because they were boyfriend-girlfriend for quite a long time, they don't want to work out on this relationship anymore.

Let's discuss about marriage issues: Whomsoever is feeling emotional, they can use their tissues.

1. Compatibility: Compatibility is not there in marriages, due to this people goes off the marriage now a days people have less patience than before so they don't want to work it out C at least you should have 50 to 70% of compatibility to labour life with somebody else.

2. Individuality: In the starting of the marriage people do so much for each other that day by day they start losing their individuality and when suddenly they start realising it, they got to know that they are not happy in the marriage or they have not thought about this, which makes a huge difference between them and that difference sometimes gets sorted out, sometime doesn't get sorted.

3. Communication: After marriage people should have communication, it is the key for every successful marriage. If you communicate more, if you share everything more, if you fight and then sort it out more, it will work out more.

4. Families: People try to adjust in different families, especially girls try to adjust in the different scenario for a different family but if the man is not supportive the adjustment is a very big thing for her. She is unable to adjust and if the man is also not supporting she gets broken at the end, and then she falls apart and then she doesn't want to make any effort for the marriage to work.

5. Only one person is trying: Marriage is a union, both should have to put in efforts towards it, only then it is going to be good, if 1% is the effort from one person and rest 99% is the effort from the other person, it will suffocate the person. You should put equal efforts towards it after marriage

also it doesn't matter if it is going to be a love marriage or an arranged marriage, effort should be equal, because now you both share a life and in this life you both share equal responsibility, equal workload, and equal happiness and sorrow; for that you have to make equal efforts so that other person will feel special about it.

6. Be Over dependent: One person is over dependent for any kind of work on another person and doesn't want to help leads to broken marriages.

7. Extra marital affairs: Nowadays extra marital affairs are so common that people are having extra marital affair after 15 years of marriage just because they don't feel that spark in their marriages, they are just chilling around and having an extra marital affair with multiple partners and think that is good, but according to me if you have work out with somebody for past 15 years you should not cheat on that person. Cheating is a thing if it is not caught it will continue and if it got caught the marriage will be broken.

For example, I have seen a person - a woman who have a very beautiful family, a very supportive husband and 20 years of marriage but now she's in her relationship with somebody else just because internally she is feeling that that person is right for her. She laughs with her husband and still feels that that the other person is also right for her and she is having a conversation with that person. Attachment with that person according to me it's just due to infatuation or crush but people are not understanding nowadays; they just think that they fall in love again and that they met their soulmate even after marriage and do such things and break their marriage, because once the trust is broken it can't come back again.

Things you should do in your marriage to spark in it up:

1. Have regular vacations; don't stick to the mundane routine, have conversations, have candle light dinners.
2. Give surprises to each other; make each other feel special at every moment of life.
3. Contribute equally in this marriage; share workload, share home workload also, one should be always calm when the other person is angry.
4. After a fight never sleep before resolving it because next day it is going to be bigger.
5. Give the other person space and time to think. You are going to have an amazing marriage then.

Confidence

Confidence is the key of success. If you have confidence and you think that confidence can survive then you should put your opinions first; you should not be afraid of the world.

You should take a stand for yourself, speak it out; don't think that anybody is going to judge you because they are judging you anyway.

If you will build confidence and positivity, you can achieve everything in life. Issues will come and go but your confidence is going to help you to conquer everything. Don't be over confident over the things but be confident about whatever decision you are going to make is going to contribute to the society and is going to be good for you.

Confidence helps us to communicate properly to tell the world what we think about, what we want to do, and to take the risk whether it is big or small. A confident person trust themselves communicate clearly ,take initiative and remain composed ,under pressure. Confidence can be internal or external, and it's often built through experience self awareness and re-silence.

3 ways to build confidence

1. Set and achieve small goals: Start with realistic and manageable coal each success boost your self believe and shows what you're capable of.
2. Practice self awareness and positive self talk: Pay attention to negative thoughts and replace them with encouraging realistic affirmations.
3. step outside of your comfort zone: Try new things, even if they are uncomfortable at first facing challenge helps you grow and prove to yourself that you can handle more than you think.

Happiness or just finding it?

Happiness is often considered an elusive concept, sometimes people spend their lives searching for. It can be found in both big moments and small moments, in achievements or in simple pleasures, in relationship or in solitude.

There is no simple key to happiness. The key to happiness lies in many things if we believe. Many believes lie in our journey of self-discovery and embracing life's ups and downs.

Rather than being a permanent state, happiness can be fleeting and situationally influenced by personal perspective and choices.

Finding happiness often involves letting go of social pressure, aligning with one true value and appreciating the present moment; ultimately it may not be about finding happiness but creating happiness by focusing on gratitude and kindness, and pursuing activities that bring joy and fulfilment to our heart.

Finding happiness in a relationship today can be both rewarding and challenging both. In our world where connections are often through technology, there is a mix of instant access to others but also potential for superficiality. True happiness in relationships comes when people are able to have deep feeling meaningful conversations and beyond the surface label conversations.

In today's fast-paced world, it's easy to get caught up in external factors like social media expectations and comparisons.

However genuine happiness in relationship comes from emotional intimacy, trust and communication along with mutual respect, where both individuals feel valued and supported. People today often seek relationship that bring out the best in them - where they can grow individually and as a couple. This means finding a balance between sharing experiences and maintaining independence. Happiness in relationships isn't necessarily about constant excitement or perfection but more about consistent sense of understanding, compromise and support through life's challenges.

In the modern world, people are also prioritising mental health and emotional wellbeing within relationships. There's an increasing awareness that happiness comes from emotional connection not just physical attraction or shared interest. Practicing empathy, being mindful of one another's needs and making time for quality moments together can also contribute to lasting happiness.

Ultimately finding happiness in relationship's today is about navigating the complexities of modern life while staying grounded in genuine connection, mutual respect and love. It's a constant effort but one that can yield great fulfilment if nurtured with care and authenticity.

Happiness for single people is often about embracing independence, self-discovery, and personal growth. While society sometimes plays emphasis on romantic relationship as the ultimate source of happiness, many single people find fulfilment in their own company, dear friendships and their personal passions.

Being single provides an opportunity to focus on one's own needs, goals and desires without the compromises and responsibility that come with a relationship.

Being single can allow for more flexibility and freedom, whether it's having more time for personal activities making spontaneous decisions or taking risk that might be difficult in a relationship.

I am not saying that you should be single, I am just telling you the benefits of being single. Ultimately happiness for single people is about realising the joy doesn't have to come from the romantic partner it can come from living authentically, nurturing close relationships and embracing the freedom to create a life that aligns with one's own desire and values.

Adjustment

What is adjustment? When you try to compromise with the situation, that is known as adjustment. Adjustment is a positive thing but too much adjustment is a negative thing.

When you are just too much, people take you for granted, they think that she will reduce we don't have to put any such kind of efforts towards her.

In marriage also, there are lots of adjustments, a girl needs to do with the partner and his family but if you have a supportive life partner these adjustments or I will say big adjustment looks little. because supportive thing works a lot.

Recently my best friend got married and she was so nervous about getting married - going into a new family and about what was going to happen after being married, but her partner is so good and so supportive that she could adjust with the family quickly.

There is an old phrase which says 'to mix like water with milk'.

If somebody wants you to adjust in each and everything that means they are just trying to take your happiness, You don't have to adjust in each and every wrong thing; if you think this thing is right and you can adjust accordingly you should adjust but if you think that's this thing is wrong and I can't adjust him this thing you should speak up for yourself.

Nobody can make you do anything until and unless you do it. Be wise. Don't be too nice. I have an example, some people are too nice that they adjust according to you in each and every situation; I know a person who was in my college, she adjusted in each and every situation and did whatever the other person would say. In the end, what happened was that people started taking her for granted that she would adjust and that she got hurt a lot. I am not saying that you should not do things in goodwill, you should do it but sometimes, trying to make other people happy isn't possible. One day you are going to just say the truth and then all the efforts will go down, so try to be as real as you can if you can't do anything just say it.

Adjustment is very good when you are in a new house - little adjustment happens in day-to-day life, that's a life thing.

Don't adjust with each and every person you don't know.

Be helpful to the people. Be truthful; as truthful as you can. Be respectful to people. Don't expect anybody to adjust for you because it is not a transactional trait that humans possess.

Mental health

Did you know that1 in 7 teenagers According to Google and 1 in 8 adults in India are suffering from mental health disorders. Yet, people are not talking so much about it. I don't know why? Have you been through suffocation?

Do you know how it feels when somebody feels anxious? When somebody feels anxious, they feel so suffocated, they feel that there is no air coming in the room, they don't feel good sitting at a place, they don't feel good walking; they are just feeling that something is happening in their body and they are just panicking out of it. This is one of the many ways in which anxiety manifests physically.

Every little thing can make them feel anxious. But because in India we don't talk about it people don't know that it is a disorder; it can be easily dealt with and they should contact as psychologist or a psychiatrist.

The suicidal rate in India is getting high day by day just because people don't know whom to talk to, about who's going to listen to them without judging them.

Mental health matters always because however you are physically fit but if you are not mentally fit and stable, then you won't be enjoying the beauty of things in life.

Depression is a disorder, it's not the lack of feeling happiness or sadness. Depressed people often struggle to make others understand what they go through. First, it must start with them being able to recognised that they need help for depression and only then will they be able to help another person about their condition.

Be empathetic towards them because they need calm. Some people in depression stop talking to other people, they just remain silent while a lot of things are going inside them. That's the key feature of depression that you are unable to discuss it with anybody because you are unable to express it.

Think how helpless it feels! When you want to express your feelings but you are unable to express it due to a disorder. These are conversations that everybody should talk about, specially to their children so that if their child someday feels the same symptoms, they talk to you their parents about it at least.

5 things you should do if you are suffering from inside or depression:

1. Talk to the nearest psychologist or psychiatrist as soon as possible; there shouldn't be shame having this disorder.
2. Meditate at least for 5 minutes a day and practice mindfulness.
3. Read motivational books and try to be surrounded by lots of people so that you don't feel alone. It's okay if you don't want to talk but at least you will be surrounded by people so you will listen to them to your over thinking process stops for a minute.
4. Practice yoga; there are so many types of yoga asanas to calm the mind.
5. Practice self-care; go for a spa or for a massage, that will make you feel calm, go for it, it will ease you down.

5 things you should avoid if you are having anxiety or depression:

1. Don't be alone all the time, don't face it alone.
2. Don't be ashamed of it.
3. If you feel like crying, cry right out; don't feel like anybody is going to judge you because it's not going to help you.
4. Don't get over attached with things or people.

5. It's okay to have mood swings; try to be calm as you can and if you can see the situation is getting worse call your psychologist as soon as possible.

Identity crisis

Identity rises is a period of self-reflection and confusion wherein individuals question themselves about the purpose and the direction of the life that they are living.

It can happen during a major life transition or during any kind of problem, at a certain age or after a personal loss.

People who are dealing with identity crisis always have a strong point of view about who I am? Why I am in this life? What is my purpose in this life?

They struggle to find it. Sometimes, identity crisis can happen in marriage also when one partner feels a loss of identity within the relationship.

This might happen when the individual begins to question who they are outside of the role of this relationship leading to a feeling of confusion surrounding their satisfaction and a sense of being unfulfilled, where there is no personal growth for them, role loss or adjustment parenthood, neglecting self-care.

In these cases, it is important to communicate clearly, reconnect with personal interest, seek support with encounter teller, find common grounds, talk it out and solve it out.

Today's students struggle with identity crises, often during the time of their age of adolescence, the transition to adulthood when they choose a career path, it's the time when the students may feel uncertain about the value they have and where they fit in the world. Is their decision is going to be right or wrong?

In these situations, my advice would be, don't think about what anybody is going to say about it. You will find the right path, you know what the right path is. You just have to find it. Meditate a little, do some self-care, and just go with the flow. You will know from your insights and you'll be successful eventually, never doubt yourself on that. Ever.

Positivity

What is positivity?

Positivity refers to the mindset or approach that focuses on a good aspect of life. It can be anything for anybody, it comes from within. Even when we face difficult times, it's all about choosing the brighter side and maintaining hope and focusing on solutions rather than being in the problem.

Being positive doesn't mean encoding challenges and pretending everything is going to be perfect, and we are going to do it, yes of course, challenges will come and you have to deal with it but with positive attitude

Key aspects of positivity are:

Gratitude: Everyone should have an attitude of gratitude about whatever we have in life.

Hope: Hope refers to maintaining our sense of optimism that things can get better and that positive outcomes are possible in difficult times also.

The ability to bounce back from setbacks and keep moving forward with confidence.

Being kind to yourself and allow room for mistakes rather than harshly criticising yourself.

How positivity impacts your well-being:

When faced with difficult problems, look for the way to resolve it not to make it more difficult.

Choose the right path rather than choosing the easier path to find the solution.

Don't ever doubt yourself; you can do it and you are going to do it.

Engage with people and you'll understand in that moment, why it uplifts and inspires you.

When negative and self-doubting thoughts arise, try to change them with more positive thoughts.

When you are in difficult times, always remember the good times you had.

Positivity when we practice daily has a significant effect on mental health, physical health, your relationship and your quality of life.

Positivity in mental health:

Positivity in the context of mental health refers to practicing of maintaining hopeful, optimistic, constructive mindset even in the face of challenges. While it's not about ignoring negative thoughts and pretending everything is perfect, it's about growing a mindset that encourages emotional well-being and healthy coping strategies.

Coping skills are the most important set of skills in mental health.

Physical health benefits:

Mental health and physical health are closely linked. Positive thinking has been shown to reduce risks of chronic illness such at heart disease, blood pressure , and diabetes mellitus.

These lifestyle disorders happen to people who don't have any kind of positivity and they are always tensed and stressed throughout their life. Thus, positivity plays a huge role in our lives, much bigger than we can imagine.

Meditation

Positive mind
Positive vibes
Positive life

As we all know, meditation is a practice that involves focusing the mind, often to achieve a state of calm, awareness and clarity. It can be done in various way, such as through mindfulness breathing exercise or visualization and most commonly to reduce stress suffocation, increase self-awareness and promote mental and emotional wellbeing.

Some forms of medications like mindfulness meditation can increased awareness of present movement, while others like transcendental meditation, use mantras, specific techniques to guide the mind, into a state of deep relaxation and focus.

Meditation techniques:

1. 2 minutes meditation technique: First sit on the floor, in a folded-legs position and let all thoughts flow, let negative thoughts come and positive thoughts come and go. If you feel like crying, you can cry aloud. If you feel like relaxing, you should relax yourself, trying to maintain your posture because it is necessary to help you breathe better.
2. 5 minutes meditation: Now focus on your breath. take a deep breath and focus on it chant the mantra om and it should be chanting like vibration that is going from your nose to the body. Chant "om" for 5 minutes.
3. Now focus on your breath and feel your breath coming and going, let the life flow with it and calm your all the senses.
4. Slowly and steadily you will begin to increase the duration of meditation and in few months, you would notice visible changes in time and the impact of it.

Everyone has own way of meditation, some do by this, some do by that, but all kinds of meditation work for the peace of mind, to understand our own self, to understand our emotions and to cut off from this stressful life.

I always say to people that whenever you feel stressful just take few deep breaths from nose and exhale from the mouth, do it 3 to 5 times and you will feel calm.

Before taking any decision, we all should do this - take few deep breaths from nose and exhale from the mouth, in this way we will be able to focus on the positivity and calmness.

Think about the situation from a different perspective and find positivity out of it and whatever your decision will be you won't be upset that you had taken it in hurry.

For example I know a person who always take decisions in hurry.

One day, that person was in front of me and there was a major life decision that the person had to take.

That person was panicking, I just asked that person to sit down, take a few breaths and that person asked me, "What are you saying? This is not going to work for me, I don't know what I'm going to say! And what decision I'm going to make! I'm so stressed, I don't know what I'm going to do to my life!"

I suggested that this person listen to me and sit down and tried to divert the conversation by asking them about a few other things. Once I noticed that this person was visibly calm, I brought back the conversation and made them make a choice. This method has been quite successful in my career.

Before the person made a choice, I said "Now you are ready to take the decision. Remember whatever decision you are going to make, it's your decision and you have to own it. Whatever the outcome will be it will be alright. You're going to do it don't worry what life is going to hold for it just to be calm and go for it."

In India, meditation has always been a part of our cultural practices, as part of exercise or otherwise as well. But in this context, we may consider this aspect of meditation to find our inner peace and strength.

Compatibility

Compatibility is an essential aspect of maintaining any relationship but people are not talking enough about compatibility in any kind of relation.

If compatibility is not there, then any kind of relationship will collapse. Nowadays, in marriages, people are more running towards financial stability, they don't see compatibility between two people. At least 50% to 60% of compatibility should be there between couples, to sustain a healthy relationship.

Due to this negligence, these relationships collapse and come to an end and they file for the divorce.

In India 1% of marriages end up in divorce due to compatibility issues but still nobody is addressing it - why? Because people are not understanding the importance of it.

In an arranged marriage setting, prospective people say compatibility will develop after marriage. But I would say no. If you don't have compatibility before marriage, then it's not going to develop after marriage after marriage. Only adjustments will happen. And after a certain amount of time, adjustments would begin to look like sacrifices and that is the beginning of the ed of the relationship.

To give you a better understanding, let us take the example of best friends; they share compatibility. In the sense that they understand what the other person would say or react in a certain situation and accordingly behave. There is a mutual understanding, cooperation and care for each other. Most importantly, there is an intention to keep the friendship afloat. These essentials can be applied to a marriage, at much more intense level.

From my perspective, everybody before getting married, either in an arranged marriage or in a love marriage, should check their compatibility with their partner - that is their compatibility or is their compatibility issue and they are adjusting about it if they think that they are these 50% of compatibility then they should go ahead. If they think that there are compatibility issues and lots of fights are happening due to compatibility and you both don't share similar interest and you both are very different people and you both think from very different perspective in life and you don't want this to continue, then you should not get married to that person.

Sometimes people get obsessed with their partner so much that they don't think about compatibility with their partner, they just want that partner to be there and after marriage when there are responsibilities that come up on their shoulders and compatibility is not there that time, they realise that their decision was wrong. Marriage is a very big decision, thus it must be taken with utmost heed.

In marriage, there is a lot of interference of family members. Thus, my two bits on this aspect is that the family too must try to not step in on the relationship because issues may only be resolved by those who face it. Advice at best, may be provided. Otherwise, the couple must try to draw thick boundaries and not give anyone the leeway to fix their marital problems.

For a single second say if you want to find a good partner for yourself first preference should be compatibility with the partner. Second thing should be financial stability. Third thing should be family and the most important thing should be empathy and sympathy that person should have.

It is essential to have these conversations around the people we love and care for, irrespective of it being romantic or a familial relationship.

If you will have compatibility with somebody, you will share your feelings and you will share everything with that person and that person will become your person. You will feel the sense of responsibility, the sense of being loved, the sense of being cared and you will feel that everything is going in the right direction. Even in the lows and ups of your life you will feel safe about it because you have compatibility with that person you will know that that person is going to trust you and that person is going to support you and understand you always have somebody to go home to.

Trust is the most important thing in any kind of relationship. If you trust your partner blindly and if you know that your partner loves you a lot, then you will be in a much more safe, secure space mentally and in the relationship.

A good life partner is definitely something that most people want. Compatibility is kind of a piece of puzzle, one person is another piece, and one person is another, together they make the puzzle. You can find compatibility at any age, you don't have to worry about being lonely.

Happily ever after with little issues

You all know that there is no happily ever after. It's just that situation gets better, issues come and go in life. So wherever you are, if you think everything is going to be happily ever after, then you are gravely mistaken and this is not a true world in true world happily ever after never exist.

Every situation gets better, you both try to understand each other and you both have a very good bonding but problems will come and you have to be prepared for it. You have to have an open mindset, you have to trust each other to face that problem with each other.

When together, you will be in a better position to take decisions together and face your problems. Then too, there are going to be smaller problems but you will be happy that you have a parent who is willing to aid you through life's journey.

'Happily ever after' is a myth but with a good, understanding partner, you may be closer to this myth and face the harsh reality at the same time.

It is true that not everyone is successful in finding the right partner at the first instance. Divorce is uncommon but the point is to try and give marriage a shot with an optimistic view. A lot of people have found later marriages to be more successful because they understand about this marriage that they have to adjust and that they have compatibility in this marriage, so they are happy about it. Issues will come in this marriage also but they will face it together because they have the compatibility.

Think from different perspectives, think positively and you will see the difference of taking decisions; you will make the right choice. Just trust yourself, trust your gut feeling.

Life from a different perspective; it's all about seeing life from different lens and pointing out different small issues of life that nobody is talking about and these small issues big issue in life after some time. You don't have to do what others are doing because you don't know if what other people are doing is right or wrong; this you have to do, what you think is right and you have to trust yourself.

You can have different perspectives, you can have different opinions, but nobody can judge you, because you have the right to speak, different opinion doesn't mean that you are wrong, it means that you are thinking from different perspective; for somebody the glass is always half empty and for somebody the glass is always half full so whose perspective is better? Nobody's; it's just that the perspectives are different, and looking through different lens is good.

Don't be ashamed of anything that you have done; just be confident and let past be past; learn from your mistakes and move forward with confidence; and do what your heart says; fulfill your desires.

You all are amazing.

With love Dr. Sana Ali.

Acknowledgements

I am author, you are a reader, and I penned this motivational book for you. But this would not have been possible without the backstage people who motivated me - the actual characters of my life - Dr. Sana's life. So I would like to thank them here.

First of all, I want to thank the universe for guiding me towards the purpose of my life.

My family and friends for their love support and trust in me. My parents have been the true inspiration for me, they always given me the confidence that I am going to give you in this book.

Special thanks to my cute, little nephew Zayn, for always having a beautiful and loving smile towards me.

I am grateful to the entire team of Blue Rose publications for their untiring effects in helping my book reach you.

www.ingramcontent.com/pod-product-compliance
Lightning Source LLC
LaVergne TN
LVHW061558070526
838199LV00077B/7101